VERTEBRAE

# VERTEBRAE

POEMS, 1978–1994

Samuel Green

EASTERN WASHINGTON UNIVERSITY PRESS

Copyright © 1994, 2008 by Samuel Green
All rights reserved.

13   12   11   10   09   08     5   4   3   2   1

*Cover illustration*: Michael Dickter, *1st Flock*
Cover and interior design by Erin T. Dodge

*Library of Congress Cataloging-in-Publication Data*
Green, Samuel, 1948–
  Vertebrae : poems, 1978–1994 / Samuel Green.
    p. cm.
  ISBN 978-0-910055-17-8 (alk. paper)
  1. Country life—Poetry. 2. Nature—Poetry. 3. Spirituality—Poetry. 4. Islands—Washington (State)—Poetry. 5. Northwest, Pacific—Poetry. I. Title.
  PS3557.R37547V47 2008
  811'.54—dc22

                                    2008034207

*Eastern Washington University Press*
*Spokane and Cheney*

*this book is for Sally,
as everything is*

*Light and praise,*
*Love and atonement, harmony and peace,*
*Touch me, assail me; break and make my heart.*

—Edwin Muir

# CONTENTS

### VERTEBRAE

Grandmother, Milking  3
Grandfather, Hauling in the Nets  5
Mussel Eating: Third Beach  6
Meditation at the Hoh River Mouth  8
Vertebrae  10
Finding the Hanged Chinaman's Grave, South Bend  12
Wind: Four Letters to Melinda Mueller  14
Mending the Instruments  21
Shaving Lesson  22
Mint Harvest, South Fork of the Nooksack  24
Sheep Turning  25
Gathering the Fruit  26
Pruning  28

### HANDS LEARNING TO WORK

Covenant: Saying Hello to the Land We Will Live With  31
Blessing  33
My Father Sang to Himself  34
Exemplar  36
Hands Learning to Work  37
Working Crosscut  38
Red Snapper  39
On Hearing Our Plans for Homesteading My Grandmother Said It Would Ruin Your Hands  40

Poem to Accompany the Gift of an Amish Rug   42
Geese in Rain   43
You Ask Me About Birds & I Tell You   44
Sitting on the Bluff Above a Bay near Home Watching
    a Woodpecker Working a Dead Snag   45
Fiddle Trees   47
Nearing Solstice   48


ROWING AGAINST THE WIND

Killing the Ground Wasps   51
Rowing Against the Wind, Against the Tide   53
Northeaster   54
"What Are We All Headed for Besides a Cold
    Grave?"   55
At the Seafarer's Memorial, Anacortes   57
There Were Deer Once   58
Mallards, Morning   60
Storm Warnings   62
David Takes His Two-Hundredth Foreskin   63
In a Borrowed House on the Mainland After the
    Blizzard   64
Bird Watching   65
Late Snow Melting, First Sign of Flowers, Gathering
    Eggs After Thinking I'd Lost You   67
Solstice, Again   69
Part of the Music   71
Ars Poetica   74
Communion   76

*Sources of Quotations*   79
*Acknowledgments*   83
*About the Author*   85

# VERTEBRAE

*These are what I see here every day,
not things but relationships of things . . .*

—Hayden Carruth

# Grandmother, Milking

On mornings when the cold
huddles in my knees & wrists
I do not understand
how I can go to sleep
& wake up in the same skin.

The women who write me
from rest homes,
I send them recipes,
songs from the old days.
When I don't hear for a while,
then I know.

I cling to the music of habits,
my hands on the old cows' teats,
the way my bad hip rises & falls
when I haul the milk pails
back from the barn, splitting
wood for the cookstove.
Patterns & rhythms.

I don't miss the other animals much,
though the miracle of a still warm egg
in the palm was something
to start a morning.

There is a garden to care for,
crops to rotate. The spuds are good
where they are, but I'll need to move
the rhubarb. Animals eat much

of what I raise. Grandpa's old clothes
hang on frames that frighten
nothing. The alarm clock
I hung from the pear tree
finds its own place in the sound
of things. Each morning the lettuce
is cropped, the bark on the branch tips
of Gravenstein & plum gnawed white. Still
I won't pay the neighbor boy to shoot
the rabbits, & the deer bring
a silence that wraps me
in sleep. I plant enough
& still do the canning. Vegetables
& meat in the freezer & jars.
Berries & other fruits sleep in their syrups.
Sometimes it's a county road crew, sometimes
a relative. I don't need to know who
will eat, only be ready if someone is hungry.
Every time I put my hands into the ground
I know what's coming out,
what's going in.

# Grandfather, Hauling in the Nets

You can pray for as many fish in the floodlamps
as stars, but you better know the water.
I learned this bottom the hard way,
these rocks tearing the heart
from my nets. Tides & currents,
too, how they'll trick a man.
Everything I want is trying to get away,
the love I wanted in my house,
what I couldn't set my nets for.
My sons, when they look at me
their eyes are as dull as these scales
drying on the deck.

I know this: a man wants something
he has to grab hold & pull hard.
My hands so hard
the jellyfish don't sting anymore.
How can a man be gentle with hands like these?

These gulf winds, the storms here
rise out of whispers, from sounds soft as the love
a man might dream about. I dream
like a fish, dream deep & heavy, dream
something's after me. You think I like
the sound of fish flapping in the hold?
How they gape? How their goddamn gills work
& work, until finally they just stop?

# Mussel Eating: Third Beach

Just at dawn the sea
enters your life. In your receding dream
she is a woman
who whispers in the whorls of your ear
a promise, the sense
of a promise, her voice
the rasp of waves
dragging back into themselves
until you stir, yawning
into the arms of a day
you can love.

It is not a July sun you wake to,
but only the sun,
warm, & no accident.
Beyond your tent the sea
quivers like a great stomach,
sigh & hiss, sigh & hiss of surf.

Time to be moving
& so you move, slipping
between the plump thighs of driftwood
onto sand, paddling naked
toward rocks exposed by low tide.

Mussels in clumps with starfish,
barnacles, eel grass, China
caps. A harbor seal bobs
like a buoy out in the chop.

The mussels, blue, you pry them loose.
A slip, & barnacles slice a neat map
in your palm. You slide your hand
into a tide pool,
wait for the cold to seal the wound.
Blood things to a pink smoke,
drifts away someplace.
Around your ankles
the suck & lick of waves.
You kneel in a skin older than you know.
What is here does not belong
to you, but you belong here,
leaning over this pool,
body curved like a petroglyph, a whale
carved on rock miles up the coast.

At camp dry cedar
for fast coals, for seawater
suddenly bubbling around the shells
which part, moist in the steam,
like the lips of a woman during love.
What you want is seabirds
rising in your chest.
Pry a mussel open, slide
its orange tongue between your lips
& the birds, the clumsy, lovely birds
lift from the fog
of your next, natural breath.

# Meditation at the Hoh River Mouth

*There's no place else: begin from where you are.*
—Theodore Roethke

I

You begin by not knowing
where you are, by just
standing & looking for landmarks.
Everything has a voice,
the rustle of crabs beneath stone,
the stones themselves. Particular
& luminous, things tilt
into vision. Pitch glistens amber
in the sun. Otter dung whitens
& dries in summer heat.

What you thought was a rock
moves, & you think *other*.
Whatever you focus on becomes
something else, moves away
from its joining.

II

Or you think you know
where you are, but direction
is iron at a compass, sound
in a thick sea fog.

Everywhere around you
there is power. Leaves
harvest sunlight. Kelp grows
a foot each day. In winter
the waves here break
at two tons per square inch.

What the eyes bring back,
what the ears & nose
trundle home—how do you fit
that in? That's what you ask
yourself, what you work toward.

III

Or you do nothing
by intention, but notice
that what normally moves
the leaves, stirs the shore
grasses, is at rest.
You think how still
everything is, & how
nothing is still, how rapidly
things move toward their becoming.

If you would own something,
give yourself to it. Move
in your place knowing your boots
rhyme with waves
the same way motion
rhymes with motion,
beginnings with beginnings.

# Vertebrae

Outside our tent
the rocks & the shadows
of rocks knit themselves
into skeletons of evening,

& the curved bone
from the spine of a whale
alone on the white log
above tideline
is dreaming
of power
depth
& the pressure
of the sea
like hands
like knowing
hands pressing, pressing,
dreaming of light, of no
light
dreaming
of connections.

We wake to the blue breath
of fire curling
into the needles
of hemlock
where light
falls through branches.

We wake
in love
with our bodies
we stretch
we open our arms
& the whole morning
rises from some deep place
arches its great back
breathes.

# Finding the Hanged Chinaman's Grave, South Bend

Most of what moves here still breathes: rabbits
hunkering in the high grass, wrens
flicking through devil's club & trees,

& me, gazing at the edge of this creek
because a man who had no luck
was hanged, & buried on a farm

a hundred years. And I have brought hot rice
as his relatives did before the place
was lost. Here for the mystery

in rituals, I watch a red kite flap
above the puffed cattails
& reeds, like a waterfowl rising

at first light, & I see nothing is more lovely
because death hovers here. Not the white
cones of blackcap or salmonberry, not

the calves stumbling beneath the swaying
bellies of old cows. It is only a place
from which to see the whole

of this place, my hip resting in the hollow
where his bones have settled. I pour
hot rice from my thermos under the tangled

roots of a fir. It steams like the mud
bank steams. No ritual. Only me moving
away across a wide field of dry

grass, watching the swallows dive
at my heels to snatch whatever
insects I disturb as I pass.

# Wind: Four Letters to Melinda Mueller

I. *From King's Garden Nursing Home*

"A shared grief is less."
She says this, an old woman
you'd like, & talks of a storm
that hit her farm in '96
a favorite cow killed
when wind crushed her father's barn
to sticks. She rocks
while I listen. Her chair clicks
on the floor like the one in your kitchen,
the one I hear each time I phone
or you do, & we share our distress.

"A shared grief is less,"
& a hard sea took her husband,
lost to his nets in rain, his body
so new to hers they hadn't time
for children.

She forgets nothing. No pain.

I listen, eyes drifting past
her face to the window. Outside
more hummingbirds than I've ever seen
whir around a feeder. Their wings
are tiny storms, move as much air
as this old woman takes in a breath.

She rocks & rocks, & speaks of death
in a Montana snowstorm, a brother. Loss.

Repeats her favorite lesson one more time.
"A shared grief is less."

She tells me this, & I tell you,
spreading it around,
increasing the strength of her flimsy lungs,
in love with the sound.


II. *From the beach at Fort Worden*

Second week of heat
& no relief from it.
At three I leave my bed
& walk to the beach
to beg for wind, a breeze
to cool the skin I feel, these days,
so out of place in.
No help. Only hug
my knees & watch the lighthouse
sweep its circle clean,
telling me the same thing my knees
tell me: I'm here, outside that light,
& it's only me hugging me.

Still I'm here at ten.
Again the sun's burned its brand
on the day. For hours now
no sounds except the rhythmic splash
of glassy swells. And still
no wind, although the air
must move: a hawk works the high
currents in a slow hunting spiral.

By the pier a mother slaps her daughter.
The child wails,
flails her arms like a windmill.
I'd guess the lady's jumpy
with the heat, hitting someone
makes it better. She sings
with her radio. It's revealing.

This letter is to say
she doesn't know what we know:
the cosmetics of healing.
We slap at nothing in our grief,
& hope that singing is enough.
The heart goes past its music,
more than beat following beat,
the surge & leap of blood
in rhythm with each pulse. In song
it's word that follows word
till something stirs. This letter,
poem, song, is yours
& meant to mend.
Say it aloud when the heat gets bad
& there you will have it: *Wind*.


III. *From Skykomish*

I can't sleep
in this place, this borrowed mattress
on the floor, noise. Close by
the river, huge with spring, makes love
to its stones. A diesel groans up the grade
toward Stevens Pass. And wind. Outside
the wind braids a rope from thick black hair,

beats the night with it, slick with rain
meant for Yakima.

Let me tell you a story.
When I was four
I saw my first storm from a logging camp
in the mountains. Gramma said strong winds
were caused when too many people
let their breaths out all at once.
All night I curled up beneath my bed, took
the smallest breaths, let them go
in slow puffs, spoke to the wind that shook
the roof, whispered, "No, this is not for you,
not for you." Morning, I climbed
into the canyon, found a fawn drowned
in a pool where the creek backed up.
Told no one for weeks, thinking
I'd helped to kill it, I was selfish to breathe.

I tell you this: we start our factories of grief early.

In anger, frustration, the fingers tuck
& roll toward the palm. Mine do that now.
I want to say something of what we do
for one another in our sadness, & don't know how.
Instead I write: *Today the wind tossed a marsh hawk
against a fence in a gust even the bird couldn't use,
broke its neck.* That bird's a look inside
the stomach of a stone. We find direction
in how we care for others when we're alone.
I sit near a window. Deer, hawk & I all hold
our breaths. Back in Seattle, you're asleep,
window open for air. Perhaps, when this wind
finally reaches you there, it will be soft,

a lover's breath, combing your hair, combing
your hair.


IV. *From Yakima*

This ridge is called *Umptanum*,
the north of two.
I am squatting
in cheat grass beside a stone
out of the wind
facing east, facing
the hills you watched
as a child, the hills
you thought were dreaming
lions, asleep on their paws,
the curves of their lives
sweeping into stories
we could read if we knew how.

I dream of stands of Douglas fir,
spruce, cedar, & hemlock,
the sense of cover. Here I feel exposed
as the rock I lean against to stop
the wind.

I am trying to *be* here,
to tell you things.

A donkey the color of dried mud
browses in cover by the road,
a flash of white in sagebrush
is the long tail of a magpie,
a yellow biplane sprays wheat

in the valley. I can feel morning
rain rising from the grass around me
into a sky swimming
with the easy weight of cumulus.

You see? It is not
that I don't know how to look.

A friend says:

*Your problem,
you want to know
what everything means,
you want reasons.*

I am full of questions.

Even the canyons here
know where they're headed,
as does the wind that sweeps
down them scattering whatever seeds
are ready. Some silences threaten,
a move into the eye of a storm.
Whichever way we turn
are winds that do not love us.

I don't know what to tell you.
The sky here is nothing
I can lean against. There are no handholds.

Beneath me there is movement
I can sense, the fine filaments,
the tangled hair of roots.

And there are days
when stones speak,
when you fill your hands
with pebbles
& they spell out a history.

Remember you said:

*Remove the tip
of a root
& it doesn't know where to go.*

Stones are good survivors.

It is no good praying
for power. It is no good
asking for help.

The water in my thermos
is so cold my eyes ache.

I leave the shelter of this rock
& step west with the wind,
flush a wren
& make myself a home
in its music.

# Mending the Instruments

*for Paul Hunter*

The banjo you fixed is one
hundred this month, & still
notes curl
into the air
from my ten fingers
like shavings under your good blades.

Great-gramma played it for the kids
on a homestead up the Dickey River
when husband & horses & wagon
never came back.

Sometimes I pick the guitar
made whole again, Grampa's
when young. Was how he made
his hands forget the axe he swung
long & long days for money. He
played, all his daughters danced.

My hands fret where theirs did.
I think of them whenever
I learn a new note, some story
their daughters taught me, practice
while my family sleeps
& the sweet patina of evening
darkens, thinking of you
mending what was broken.

## Shaving Lesson

I hand over the bone-
handled razor, German,
the stone wrapped in oilcloth
& the horsehide strop.

He is ninety, nearly
blind, & does not
know me. Only he is
pleased I want to learn
how men have done this act,
mindful of tools that
others have grown old
using.

I give him my stiff brush
of pig bristles, white mug,
a cake of fresh soap.

What I expect
is that he will cut me.
And I am right: a tiny nick
just under the left ear.

The quick blood wells up, runs
down my neck. The same blood
goes back four fathers before
my own, the men who owned
these tools, passed them on
to a son, a grandson

who sits in a chair with a mirror
worn smooth by another man's
holding.

# Mint Harvest, South Fork of the Nooksack

Tea drinking, the song
of the river dried in leaves
& pale blossoms
flowing as they swell
& all morning pours
from the cup between my hallowed hands.

## Sheep Turning

Green hills in a country
not my own, morning
& evening the rancher
& I followed his lively collie
through acres of stony pasture.
He'd bark at sheep dense with wool
& helpless as turtles.

I'd leap off the truck, muscle
them up, watch them amble away
always toward water. Sometimes
they'd stumble again, the weakest ones.

Broad-winged birds circling
the scorched air showed us
where we were late.

For this I got room & board
thirteen years ago, New Zealand.

But just now, pulling squash
from their frightful leaves,
I realize that still I am looking
for sheep, that always I've sought
the still shape too far gone
to bleat, working my arms
around for the best grip, whispering
*I'm glad I found you, I'm so glad I found you.*

## Gathering the Fruit

*for Jody Aliesan*

Last season, despite
my wanting, three apples
on the highest branches.
Now, the heart of an Indian summer,
limbs sag beneath the weight
of ripening.

Despite neglect, my failure to prune,
the branches bend low & I bend
under them, gathering the fruit
into my shirt, picking from grass
I would not mow, loving its thickness.

Maybe the bees
have done something. Things come
anyway. They come to us.

These, with their dark bruises,
for canning, for thick clouds of juice.
These, bird-scarred, for drying
on strings above the woodstove.
How we save against
thin times. I smell apples
before biting. My grandmother
taught me, white pulp sweet on
the tongue, wet.

Some fall in the garden. Zucchini
still growing here, sweet squash. Their broad
leaves breathe quietly in this air
that strains to be morning. Apple
cores, peels, seeds, leaves when
they drop—mulch for these
& other crops. Next year wild
mint, I think, & herbs.

Each day I do
this simple work, expect
nothing, take nothing
from the branch, bow,
reap only what falls.

# Pruning

Whatever doesn't bear fruit
blocks light, strays
from the center, draws
too much life from the limb.

With tools I filed myself
I cut these clean from the body,
tie them into bundles to burn
in a fire I kneel before.
How we learn.

# HANDS LEARNING TO WORK

*A man knows when he has found his vocation when he stops thinking about how to live and begins to live.*

—Thomas Merton

# Covenant: Saying Hello to the Land We Will Live With

We pace off boundaries in a light rain
wondering whether the air
slips over us or we slip
into the air. We have only
the compass of how we walk here
how our feet move
over the soil that will feed us.

Everywhere there are gestures
of welcome: the intricate calligraphy
of branches, the slow traffic of summer
birds, the million plants giving up
their oxygen, our lungs filling.

There was the voice in your head the first time
we came

*I will die here*

like a benediction, light as the first leaf
fall, & you unafraid.

I watch you kneel & smell
a handful of soil, the cornerstone
of wonder. The elements
of a future assemble inside us
though we worry where the water is,
whether we can build before
winter, how to find the longest light
for the labor we will do here.

Neither of us speaks it

> *I will stay with you*
> *here, here I will love you*

made good by the doing,
a contract signed & witnessed
with each breath as we keep faith
with the land, the names
we will learn, passing into each season
passing through in turn.

# Blessing

Bless what sprang from egg or seed.
Bless what stayed & drew in light.
Bless what moved upon the earth & breathed.
And bless, bless this: that what we eat
we eat from need.

# My Father Sang to Himself

Sometimes my father sang
to himself in the woods.
I could see
his lips move, the howl
of the chainsaw nearly hiding it.

He'd stop
when he saw me coming
down the trail he'd cut
through stinging nettles & blackberry.

Sometimes he sang for me
leaned against a new stump
while the smell of sawdust mingled
with black coffee I brought
for him, familiar songs, not
the strange tunes I never heard twice.

Sometimes
at the sewing frame
or swinging an axe
sometimes handling a hoe in the garden
I rest
& know I've been singing.

But I cannot bring back
that music,
cannot sing to you here what
still lingers somewhere
in the charged, the altered air

communal
the breath of work
coming in, the song
flowing
out.

# Exemplar

When the old-timers cleared
their fields for the plow
they sometimes found boulders
too big for horse & skid. They
covered these over with brush
& waited for weather
safe enough to burn, then lugged
seawater in buckets up the steep bluff
from the beach & poured it
over the hot rock
which would rapidly hiss,
contract, & split.

They did this
again & again, until the stones
were small enough
to manage. These they hauled or
tossed to the boundaries of their lives'
work, the seeds they broadcast
with their best faith upon
the turned earth against the coming
push of frost.

# Hands Learning to Work

Sunrise near the house site pigeons
flush from thick elderberry, a dozen bandtails
drumming into the cedar grove our bedroom
will overlook. Chill air, logs slick

with dew. My caulked boots grip
a peeled pole as I balance on the west wall,
start a new notch. *Good tools don't mean
good work, beyond the work that made them,*

but these fit my hands: a hand-turned dogwood
maul, a hand-forged fishtail gouge. Each rap
means a slice of fir from the log, onion
thin. Though the birds & the fat red berries

mean it's June, & already the log walls lean
toward fall in my mind, though something in me,
too, straddles the honed edge of alarm, I move
slowly, deliberate, for the doing & not to be done,
hands learning to work from the work at hand.

# Working Crosscut

All around me third-growth white fir
finds a way from sandy soil
through the logging slash
I'm sawing up for fuel.

With a crosscut you can hear
things. That rustle in snowberry
is a winter wren. A pileated
woodpecker works the dead tip
of a Douglas fir, his read head a noisy blur.

I rest more often than the woodpecker,
regard the buds of elderberry
swelling, the smell
of wood wet from last night's rain.

When I start again, rocking
the long blade as my father
taught me, the rhythm's almost
the same as the wing
flap of a passing crow, & then
there's the first soft crack
as the heart of the log sags,
breaks, & lets go.

# Red Snapper

A three-foot carcass sprawled
in the gut bucket
at the West Beach dock.
Fresh. We watched the tourist
toss it there, & beat the flies.

Now it steams on the wood range
beside a pan of peppers
& thin-sliced garlic. With garden greens
the three of us should eat two days.

Do we bless the hand
that cleaned the fish so poorly,
the man who said the fish are gone,
too many predators,
that we should shoot the seals?

We curse his luck, his boat, his bait & line,
we serve the flaking meat & solemnly begin our meal.

## On Hearing Our Plans for Homesteading My Grandmother Said It Would Ruin Your Hands

After a long year & the gestures
of several seasons, your hands
have learned
how to be lovely.

Small, so thin. I take them
in mine & taste the many loaves
of bread pushed & shoved & kneaded,
smears of chicken blood, the feathers
clinging. They cramped
beneath the goat's full udder
one morning. I warmed them
with steam from my breathing.

Red welts from the cookstove, skin
cracked at the washboard,
raw in January wind. Axe scars,
knives, the pale prints of too many
knives. Nails chipped
with the cycles of seeding,
the stubborn roots of weeds.

And what shall I say of the birds
that live in your hands? Swallows
in them, sparrows &
delicate wrens. Each night they
roost & murmur their long
sleep songs in my body.

Calluses now, tough horn
on these palms I've never seen
clenched in anger, gentle
with what they hold, with what they could
hold, lovely
with work that's made them stronger.
My hands, too, how they
linger.

# Poem to Accompany the Gift of an Amish Rug

*for Sally*

Here is affection born of care, the lines
of a well-kept garden & fields
cleared of stone. Here
are the sighs of animals tended
in their turn, the filled hours
of evenings before rest, the braids
of silent prayer.

You can believe the woman who made this
believed the message of her hands,
that if you live well, you work well
& the only sin is separation. Spread
on the floor by our bed, it is something
on which we both can stand.

# Geese in Rain

*after a Chinese painting*

There are nine shapes making a way
through strong wind, judging
by the slant of the long lines
of rain, & the stretch of their necks.

Is the leader tiring,
giving way to those behind?

There is no way to know
whether we are greeting them
in spring rain, or
saying farewell in the fall
wondering which &
how many will return.

Either way
we have to let them go.

# You Ask Me About Birds & I Tell You

if, sometimes, when a heron
spread her great wings to dry
in whatever sun there was, I
thought of you, the hidden strength
unfolding from your body,

& if, watching hawks work
through air so still only the sunlit tips
of their wings moved, like fingers,
I remembered the tips of your fingers
in their slow love circles, oh

yes, & if I've noticed
how a raven's wings luff
overhead like spilled breath,
how an owl's scoop air without sound
in its quickest flight,

it was to understand this,
our coming together, the way
pine siskins leave a tree, suddenly, all
at once, & between their startled wings
those drunken patches of light.

# Sitting on the Bluff Above a Bay near Home Watching a Woodpecker Working a Dead Snag

Clearly this is a favorite tree,
pocked with holes new made
& others weathered gray.

Looking for one more stray
blind grub the bird rips
an old wound rapping

a hollow music, stops,
cocks an eye to see if I watch,
chatters, flies off, back, scatters

splinters of dry wood
that float around the trunk
like termite wings.

Gaudy bird, head like a red-lacquered box,
I want to heave a rock at him.
Better to face the rain & wind

for whatever's to be found there,
like the still shape against the cliffs
across the bay, a heron the color

of shaded stone, wind ruffling the long feathers
at its neck. Silent, shy as a Chinese hermit
poised at the tidal edge,

it waits for a single swirl of motion, that brief
flicker of light followed by the one quick thrust
which is almost always true.

## Fiddle Trees

Hiking back late from a dance,
full moon brushing the shoulder
of the ridge, new snow
light on the ground, we pause
along the trail to listen
at the sound two close-grown cedars make
rubbing in a random breath of air.
*Fiddle trees*
my grandfather called them.

How long do we stand there? Enough
to take that music
into our own limbs for the quick walk
home, the long night's steady hum.

## Nearing Solstice

December dusk, a great horned owl appears
at the top of old-growth cedar. We cup
our mittened hands around our mouths & hoot
& cannot know she hears, but then she calls,
her body bowing forward with each note
& from the four directions, from the great cross
of stars, come all the answers, all
the answering throats.

# ROWING AGAINST THE WIND

*But for each man
There is a real solution, let him turn from himself and man to love
God. He is out of the trap then. He will remain
Part of the music, but will hear it as the player hears it.*
—Robinson Jeffers

*If you are a religious man without a religion, you're in trouble.*
—William Everson

# Killing the Ground Wasps

Each day brings its work. This one
brought rain & the promise of fall
in the day's chill. All morning I
burned slash in the safe damp
cleaning my land before stumbling
into wasps, their fury,
hot pain in my legs.

After dusk, by the dying
brushfire's glow, I find the swept hole
of a nest near the upflung roots of a
deadfall, & spill in half
a canning jar of coal oil.

When the sound begins, it's a low
hum, then a buzz that grows
in the resonant ground. Almost
I think the cries rise through the soles
of my shoes. Two thousand wings,
fanning alarm, try to clean
the air, become a long exhaling moan
that dies, collapses
into itself the way they say the universe
will finish: a black hole of silence.

How do we prepare for this inheritance?
Even a simple act recalls
the Horror. And when I turn to step
past the slumbering fire, nothing

follows after. Only days,
& not desire, can wear the smell
of coal oil from my hands.

# Rowing Against the Wind, Against the Tide

Tony called this a sweet boat &
it is. The nine-foot oars swing clean
in their locks, cut deep, bring all the weight
of the bay back to my shoulders until pain
eddies in my back & neck. I was halfway
to the dock when the sun smeared its faint
tinge of blood across the trees on Stuart Island.
Tide at full flood. Wind from the southeast.
In this dark I could be moving still,
I could be rowing in place.

Last night, when the first thunderclap broke
over the island, my son woke crying
*bomb* & in his half sleep believed
I lied when I told him no. As tight
as I could I held him, the taste
of tears in my mouth, his fearsweat
on my lips when I kissed him. If
it comes, that storm will come
from the south: *Bremerton  Boeing  Bangor*

After a wind like this, there will be seaweed
on the beach, & neighbors with forks
for the harvest. Sweat cools my wool
watchcap. Each blister means a new callus
forming, pain before the strength
of the next pull. In the chop I keep
the stern lined up with a splash of lamp light
on the point, moving into the night
ahead, its uncertain length.

## Northeaster

Kate sweetens in a cold snap.
The last of the Oregon grape
swells & splits with its sugary pulp.

Seasoned alder splits with a clean pop
rattles in the arms
like dry bones
in a wind across the tundra.

## "What Are We All Headed for Besides a Cold Grave?"

*—a neighbor*

We are headed toward fall, toward
the orchard where frantic wasps
burrow into apples & the fat hips of pears,
toward the first frost & winter
following, cold & the rats in the brush
grown hungry.

Last night we covered the blameless tomatoes.

Already the sun in our minds
arcs low, & thick trees block
the light. We are moving toward long nights,
the soft glow of lamps lit early, & early to bed.

We are moving toward rain & the slow
pace of work that will not wait
for easy weather, toward earned rest
where we dream over seed catalogs littering
our table like leaves tossed on the compost.

Out on the point a sheep is dying, too weak
to rise, to raise its head. Over the winter
we will watch its carcass melt into rock, patches
of wool catching in thorns along the trail,
blowing over the cliff's edge & the sea
in winds that shape the bay.

Each evening we scrub away earth
from the gardening, pitch from the woodshed,
ink & paste from the making of books
& move toward each other. In love
we move toward love, even toward the grave
that waits us, warm with our bodies'
breaking down.

## At the Seafarer's Memorial, Anacortes

A storm beyond the breakwater
snatches foam from wave crests,
lifts a paper sack from the top
of a stuffed litter barrel, & scrapes it
across the parking lot.

Fenders of the purse seine fleet moan against their floats.
Crows in the rigging hunker against the cold.

In the parking lot a man & wife check
their stretched-out nets for tears. They
nod to a woman who's stooped to pray
at the name of her son.

Wind wears another year from the marble,
& two gray gulls are lost against a gray sky.

## There Were Deer Once

Dawn, the morning chores just
done, & I am picking the last
of a season's blackberries
for breakfast, working my way down a path
hacked through slash left
by careless loggers.

The thick brush hides fruit
wet with mist from midsummer fog.
My wrists get scratched
despite care,
& my clumsy groping
makes me wish
for deer, their special grace
a watcher shares
for the time of watching.

There were deer once.
They swam the fast currents
between islands, slept
or browsed maybe near
some of these malformed cedars
the loggers left.

A man named Briggs had dogs
trained to worry a deer
from the trees, harry it
to the beach into green waves
that stroked its knees while he
took the slow, the safe, the easy

shot. Did he wonder
when the puzzled dogs stayed
silent in the woods? There had been so
many, he must have thought
they would last forever, he
must have watched
always, must have listened for
what became only an absence stepping
its shadowed way
through a dense thicket of years.

This morning he'd see
the tracks of tethered goats
that might trick the longing eyes
for an instant, could hear
how the heavy mist magnifies
the drone of supertankers
hauling their black freight
through Boundary Pass. The foghorn
on Saturna's east point moans
its grave warning. I move with care
among seedling fir, weave my stained fingers
through damp berry vines & the fragile
webs of field spiders. Touch
any strand, & the vibration,
the disturbance, is felt
everywhere.

## Mallards, Morning

When the hound flushed the first
round of mallards from the marsh

I was saying something about guilt,
that tangled nest of old shadows

& I thought how exact those frantic
wings fit what I know of how

fear rises in me sometimes. The birds
flew off across a frost-held field

toward the bluff & two eagles circling
the drift logs below. You faced

into the wind to watch, your eyes
misting with the cold. Or perhaps

you were thinking of our neighbor
the day before, watching his two sons

fly off in a plane to their mother. We
held him as he wept, & he shook in our arms

while you stroked his hair.
I was about to say something more

about fear when our dog moved again
& more mallards rose, & again, four

separate risings. The water from their
bellies make a fine mist over cattails

& salt grass, empty nests
of marsh wrens, the stick mounds

of muskrats, & on the pair of us,
grinning like two fools set free.

I think we were already
thinking of home & the trail

where we'd hear, as our hands held
the wild rose thorns aside

for each other's passing, the landing
*shhhhhh* of the safe, the utterly

safe ducks, under the eyes of those birds
who choose well & mate for life.

## Storm Warnings

I'm at a kitchen table, describing how
I watch the barometer, how I
keep a weather log every day to compare
events & symptoms later. I'm learning
to watch birds, I say, & what it means
when wind moves from the crowns
of trees into the undergrowth, lifting
what's usually protected. It's
fascinating, I say, & would keep on
except the youngest woman at the table,
who's kept her face down, says, *You
want to know what I study? His eyes,
& where they go. If they follow me
around the room for a long time,
even when I'm doing the small,
unimportant stuff, then
I know what's coming, I know
I gotta watch out.*

# David Takes His Two-Hundredth Foreskin

This man is more dear to me than Saul:
open enemy, & strong. He keeps me a warrior.

Like the desert, the sand-scoured rocks,
the blades of wind sharp as the stone

I use to slice away the flaps of skin
that cover this flimsy crown. Saul's crown

no longer fits him. One need not use
one's strength to match deceit; it can be met

with itself. But I have met it in the open.
Saul's daughter will open to me soon,

& when my fingers grip the harp, when I sing
of God, who made the desert, the wilderness

from which we make ourselves, when I sing for us all,
I'll sing to this man, too, & his brothers, but not for Saul.

## In a Borrowed House on the Mainland After the Blizzard

All afternoon a doe browses
the clearing in front of the house
stepping among thorns
& wind-flattened grasses
for whatever is still tender.

When we open the door
for firewood, she stays
at her work, glancing at us
merely. I pass
the window coming to you shirtless
in a room charged with her peace
& she does not startle, twitch,
or even shift her eyes.

# Bird Watching

*for Howard Aaron*

We came for that, to mark the small shapes
perched in brush & high grass, to gather names
one by one, to make a nest of names.

From that steep knob of hill our glasses
scooped the bowl of Wenas Valley clean,
fields, thickets, & invisible rivers

of air. The birds were there. We heard songs
from all sides, but couldn't catch as much
as a single flicker of motion.

That night the lights of Yakima failed
in a storm. Lonely, a week from our wives,
we sat near a window in the dark

& drank warm whiskey while beaked lightning
tore at the rabbit-hunched hills,
too quick for us always.

Ten years ago, & now a man I've followed
all morning says we were wrong,
that it's not so much to watch

as listen, that each song bears a name.
He stops at every phrase & labels its maker:
*Thompson's Warbler, Swainson's Thrush, Bewick's Wren.*

To sight the bird is merely confirmation.
Ten years. I've learned enough
to think he, too, is mistaken. That day

on the hill we should have flopped on our backs
& let the songs come, never mind the names,
let the notes wash over us like syllables of rain

as though we were fields, or the thirsty dust
of hills, ignored the lightning bolt, alert
for whatever the brief & lonely light revealed.

# Late Snow Melting, First Sign of Flowers, Gathering Eggs After Thinking I'd Lost You

> *Grief, too, is work that has to be done.*
> —Anne Pitkin

Sometimes in the night, smothered
under too many blankets, I wake
from a black sleep & lie
shaking against the curve of your back
while two owls call in the close cedars.
Only the need for work draws me up to light
lamps & the two fires, fetch water,
& answer the quarreling chickens.

Sometime in the night, the wind changed
direction, warmed, & now the trees drip
with a March snowmelt that sounds,
on the roof, like rain. Outside I scatter
scratch & grain for the hens & see
near their pen, the first mud-splattered green
shoots of daffodils. They must have been
there yesterday beneath new snow
when we took the trail into woods burdened
under sudden weight, ducked through
young firs bowed & broken,
through chokecherry, through fishbone alder.

Smoke lifted from the doctor's chimney
so that her door opened at our knock. I waited
while you talked, while you placed her hand

where you pressed mine only an hour past,
the soft slope of your left breast,
a hidden lump firm under my fingers.
*It's nothing* she said *nothing
dangerous I don't know what it is*

We drank tea, then followed our tracks
back home, dumb with the gift
of one another, cold fists in our lungs.

I had not understood love
is a kind of grief. It was your name on my tongue
cracked the shell of nightmare, my hands
screaming *cancer* wherever they touched,
frantic as these hens scratching snow-patched
earth, backing off, eyes cocked for anything
that moves. How is it possible to see
these daffodils break through muddy ground
& not think how the bulb that will bloom
into our deaths may even now be sprouting in us?

So I gather eggs. Small
miracles, they make me weep. Last fall
a broody hen sat on a nest for weeks
while egg after egg exploded
beneath her until only the last one hatched,
the chick an owl killed later.

What is there to do but try again,
turn these to the light for the hidden blood
spot? They're what I can bring you, & the news
of flowers starting under a skin
of snow, the coming spring, morning's work begun.

## Solstice, Again

*for Alicia Hokanson*

One more day the hours of light fall away
too fast, & we are folded
into a frosty darkness, the moon bruised
with clouds, & an Arctic wind sweeping
south. Only the chimes beneath the eaves
lighten the chill. It is for you I stand
in our clearing tonight to scan the sky
for signs, stars glittering like sand
on the wing of a raven. Once, I believed
I could connect the dots
of light into whorls & behold
the thumbprint of God. Now I
turn away from Praesepe,
low out of sight to my left,
& there is Altair perched
in cedars to the west, above it
the Arrow, & the stars of the Lyre,
as much a sign as I'm likely to get.

Three times, say the Hopi,
the world was destroyed—by fire,
ice, the last time by flood—
& then remade, held
for The People hidden away.

When the waters were gone they were stopped
by an eagle who guarded the door.
Were they worthy of the world? Could they pass
a test? Kokopilau

stepped forward, the humpbacked flute player.
Stooped beneath his load
he raised his flute & played.

Eagle listened, then drew
a well-made bow & pierced
the player with an arrow. Still
the notes of the flute changed
the air, floating like ash,
like snow, like a sweet rain
dissolving the shaft & rinsing
the sharp wound clean.

So The People passed into sunlight.

And what does this say to us?
That we sing despite pain or in spite of it?
Tomorrow the surgeons will come with their knives,
while you sleep they will take something from you.
Tomorrow the fever of darkness
will break, & again we are given the choice,
how to honor the gift of what light we have.
It bends us, & binds us
together. Though each day the planet
is unmade around us, hours dividing
like the cells of your cancer, we sing it whole again,
mortaring one hope to another, moment by moment,
earning a way back into the world.

## Part of the Music

*When great Nature sighs, we hear the winds*
*Which, noiseless in themselves,*
*Awaken voices from other beings,*
*Blowing on them.*
*From every opening*
*Loud voices sound. Have you not heard*
*This rush of tones?*

—Chuang Tzu

I was trying to pray
moments before I dropped
the bowsaw, stopped work
mid-stroke & let it fall, fell
myself onto patched knees
beside the work-scarred sawbuck
into mud & rotting leaves.

Our lives catch up with us.
I thought I could bless mine,
stack up grace like a cord of seasoned wood.
"Live like a poet," a poet said, "you'll
write like one." I thought I had done
with the world, could live on an island
where work & love would be enough.
For more than a year it was,
clearing land, learning the way
of animals & tools, building a house.
Finally, I wanted my neighbors to be more
than they were, thinking I was.

Once, I went to church
with a Catholic friend & because I was a boy
& didn't know, I sat while all the rows
kneeled like field grass swept
by wind. The woman behind me slapped
the back of my head, she cursed
at me to kneel & pray. I did,
& prayed she wouldn't hit me.

This time my own hand
brought me to my knees
in the failing light
of a day in late fall
staring past my own vomit at a rusting saw.
I set those teeth
with secondhand tools, ground them true
as my wife's love until it was a joy
to put by wood for the fire, a pleasure
that wore away until everything was flailing
with a dull file.

How, without faith, do you pray
for faith? My brother, born again,
calls it *the divine zap* come undeserved.
"A man cannot hate the world
without hating himself," a poet said.
Six years of self-obsession. Birds
for which I had no names
had gone, their absence unsayable,
known then only by their missing songs
under a wind rising & rising
like a bucket of pain
from grief's deep well.

It wasn't the first time.
I would have gotten up, scuffed
leaves over what I had left
of myself in the mud, picked up
the saw & gone back to my labor
but for a stray gust
that just then spilled
from the hill's crest. Wind
makes a different sound
through cedar & hemlock, fir & maple,
alder & yew. I'd learned
to separate the sounds, naming them to friends
as though names mattered & not the one
voice out of many, *at-one-ment*, what binds
us finally. Hauling my load
of wood & tools back toward the house I'd made,
I heard the whole wind
that breathes through us all, each
part of the music, & the silence after.

## Ars Poetica

*for Sam Todd, 1903–1990*

Nothing I might do could keep the seals
from sliding off their rocks,
their wave-worn ledges
& into the water. To spot them there
is half gift, half the simple trick
of being ready to see.

I cannot row silently enough
to surprise them, & now we are in
the shallow channel between two
small islands, boulders
close under our hull. My son
in the stern is scared
we might hit something, caught
as we are in the suck
of ebb tide. The rocks

are a bird refuge, & the gull stench
spreads over us
like a heavy wing
in the day's heat. A few seals
bob among the bull kelp, wide-eyed
& wary, even as I struggle
to keep the bow straight
in the current. I've seen their look
before, when my grandfather
drove my brother & me over truck
roads in the Olympics above Grisdale,

a company town where he worked
as a cat skinner. His language sketched
the landscape beyond the windshield:

*shot a buck along this road once
still got some in the freezer*

*see thet cedar stump? thew a track
offa the D-8 right there  Lord God
foreman thew a fit  I hadta laugh*

*hey  ain't thet a funny snag? a fahr
few years back did thet  you hafta watch it*

And right then, deer—three does a hundred yards
past the snag—alert, gazing at us. Twice
it was elk browsing huckleberry. A black bear
clawing grubs from a log. And once only
a bobcat crouched on a limb above the river,
its eyes fixed & fiery. Always the litany
of landmarks before the animal, always
my grandfather's silent grin at our joy,
his own eyes on the road ahead, strong hands
at the wheel. My son leans over the gunwale
imagining rocks tearing the hull & doesn't see
the minke whale surface, blow, & roll
under, leaving a vapor that rainbows
briefly in the sun. With my grandfather's voice
I say, *What kind of boat is that
toward Sandy Point?* as we enter a tidal lee,
& my boy turns to look, surrounded
by the shy seals
he thought we came to see.

# Communion

Grandmother, here
is the Gravenstein,
gift of a friend on our moving.
Last year its first full crop. I felled
an old cedar I loved
to let in the light, chopped out
the nettles. Here,

Grandmother, in space we cleared
nine years with hands & fire,
from the oldest gardens on this island,
rhubarb & hops, oregano & thyme,
the long vines of marionberries,
all of them grown from starts.

I remember your neighbors,
walking with you the distance
between kitchens to visit another who knew
what a garden meant once—
putting things up,
keeping the family together—dead now,
their farms divided for taxes.

We bought this fig & plum from a nursery.
They've come through the coldest winter
we've had. The soil here is sandy. We've
changed it with compost & bartered manure,
with seaweed I hauled in our cart,
cleared the rocks. So much you taught
me, that the difference between seed & stone

is hope, Grandmother, what a danger
nostalgia is, like strands of barbed wire
in the hay I forked to the milk cows
for you when I could, small boy
& youth, & after the dark time
of my early manhood. Here,

where I work with my wife
in ways your own husband wouldn't,
I dreamed I bent near each of the plants
with a pinch of something. I could hear
my joints crack as I stooped
above one of your roses, a gooseberry
bush, raspberries, & five kinds of mint
that steeped for me once on your range,
all I asked for when you died,
when the stroke unraveled you
like the ball of leftover baling twine
by the rug you were hooking. Now,

beside one of your herbs
that even my botanist neighbor can't name
nor you whisper
from the ashes I spread near its roots,
I begin to bring you back
to us. By the rose & the gooseberry
I crumble the charred bones of your hands
through my fingers. I give you
to plum & apple, Grandmother, to the welcoming
soil, you canning jars clean on our shelves
& waiting.

## SOURCES OF QUOTATIONS

p. vii

>                    Light and praise,
> Love and atonement, harmony and peace,
> Touch me, assail me; break and make my heart.

> Edwin Muir, from "Soliloquy," in *Collected Poems of Edwin Muir* (New York: Grove Press, 1957), p. 172.

p. 1

> These are what I see here every day,
> not things but relationships of things . . .

> Hayden Carruth, from "The Ravine," in *From Snow and Rock, from Chaos: Poems, 1965–1972* (New York: New Directions, 1973), p. 20.

p. 8

> There's no place else: begin from where you are.

> Theodore Roethke, from "The Dance of the One-Legged Man," in *Straw for the Fire* (New York: Doubleday, 1972), p. 67.

p. 29

> A man knows when he has found his vocation when he stops thinking about how to live and begins to live.

> Thomas Merton, *Thoughts in Solitude* (New York: Doubleday Image Book, 1968), p. 85. Originally published New York: Farrar, Straus, and Cudahy, 1958.

p. 49

> But for each man
> There is a real solution, let him turn from himself and
>   man to love
> God. He is out of the trap then. He will remain
> Part of the music, but will hear it as the player hears it.

> Robinson Jeffers, from "Going to Horse Flats," in *The Selected Poetry of Robinson Jeffers* (New York: Random House, 1938), p. 583.

p. 49

> If you are a religious man without a religion, you're in trouble.

> William Everson, from "The San Francisco Poets: An Interview with David Meltzer and Jack Shoemaker," in *Naked Heart: Talking on Poetry, Mysticism, and the Erotic* (Albuquerque: University of New Mexico Press, 1992). Originally published in *The San Francisco Poets* (New York: Ballantine Books, 1971).

p. 67

> Grief, too, is work that has to be done.

> Anne Pitkin, personal communication

p. 71

> When great Nature sighs, we hear the winds
> Which, noiseless in themselves,
> Awaken voices from other beings,
> Blowing on them.

From every opening
Loud voices sound. Have you not heard
This rush of tones?

> Thomas Merton, "The Breath of Nature," in *The Way of Chuang Tzu* (New York: New Directions, 1965).

p. 71

Fastidiously, keep your body clean. Live
like a poet you'll write
like one.

> Olga Broumas, from "Five Interior Landscapes," in *Soie Sauvage* (Port Townsend, WA: Copper Canyon Press, 1979), p. 9.

p. 72

A man cannot hate the world and his own kind
without hating himself.

> Wendell Berry, from "A Secular Pilgrimage," in *A Continuous Harmony* (New York: Harcourt Brace Jovanovich, 1975), p. 11.

ACKNOWLEDGMENTS

Grateful acknowledgment is made to the editors and publishers of the following, where some of the poems in this collection, sometimes in slightly different versions, have appeared:

*The Alaska Quarterly Review, The Arts* (a publication of the King County Arts Commission), *The Bloomsbury Review, Longhouse, The Montana Review, Oregon East, Poetry Northwest, Poetry NOW, Potlatcxh, Prairie Schooner, Rain in the Forest, Light in the Trees: Contemporary American Poetry from the Northwest,* ed. Rich Ives (Missoula, MT: Owl Creek Press, 1983), *The Seattle Times, The Seattle Voice, Willow Springs, Working the Sea: An Anthology of Northwest Writing,* ed. Finn Wilcox and Jerry Gorsline (Port Townsend, WA: Empty Bowl Press, 1986), *Working the Woods, YELLOW SILK: Journal of Erotic Arts,* and *ZYZZYVA*.

Many of these poems were also published in the following chapbook collections:

*Communion* (Seattle: Grey Spider Press, 1992), *Vertebrae* (Seattle: Grey Spider Press, 1989), *Hands Learning to Work* (Waldron Island, WA: Brooding Heron Press, 1984), *Keeping Faith* (Seattle: Grey Spider Press, 1980), and *Wind: Four Letters to Melinda Mueller* (Portland: Breakwater Press, 1980).

In addition, "You Ask Me About Birds & I Tell You" appeared on the *Northwest Poets & Artists 1991 Calendar*, produced by the Bainbridge Island Arts Council, "Grandfather, Hauling in the Nets" was included in "Cotton Nails," a set of broadsides from Blue Begonia Press, and "Poem to Accompany the Gift of an Amish Rug" was issued as a broadside by Mad River Press.

The author would like to thank certain individuals for their encouragement during critical times in the very long and often painful development of the manuscript for this book:

Howard Aaron, Winnie Adams, Jody Aliesan, Nelson Bentley, Hayden Carruth, Phyllis Ennes, Bob Gamble, Donald Hall, Paul Hansen, Robert Hedin, Alicia Hokanson, Paul Hunter, Lonny Kaneko, Dave Lee, Denise Levertov, James McAuley, Tim McNulty, Bill Ransom, Kim Stafford, and Barry Sternlieb.

Very special thanks are due to Chris Stern, the editor and publisher of Grey Spider Press, for his friendship and faith. The debt is unpayable.

ABOUT THE AUTHOR

Samuel Green grew up in Anacortes, Washington, and has lived nearly all his life in the Pacific Northwest. After joining the U.S. Coast Guard at the age of seventeen, he saw service first in Antarctica and later in South Vietnam. He went on to earn his MA in English from Western Washington University through the Veterans Vocational Rehabilitation Program. The author of ten poetry collections to date, Green has been a visiting poet at colleges in Utah, Wyoming, and Washington and is active with the Skagit River Poetry Festival. He currently teaches poetry at Seattle University, both on the Seattle campus and as part of a summer studies abroad program in Ireland.

In December 2007, Green was named Washington State's first Poet Laureate. "Sam's passion for poetry is contagious," said Kris Tucker, executive director of the Washington State Arts Commission, "and he will share his enthusiasm with people across the state." He lives in a hand-built log house on Waldron Island, where he and his wife, Sally, own and operate the award-winning Brooding Heron Press and Bindery.